Cambridge Discovery Readers

Level 2

Series editor: Nicholas Tims

Grandad's Magic Gadgets

Helen Everett-Camplin

CAMBRIDGE
UNIVERSITY PRESS

CAMBRIDGE
UNIVERSITY PRESS

University Printing House, Cambridge CB2 8BS, United Kingdom

One Liberty Plaza, 20th Floor, New York, NY 10006, USA

477 Williamstown Road, Port Melbourne, VIC 3207, Australia

314–321, 3rd Floor, Plot 3, Splendor Forum, Jasola District Centre,
New Delhi – 110025, India

103 Penang Road, #05-06/07, Visioncrest Commercial, Singapore 238467

Cambridge University Press is part of the University of Cambridge.

It furthers the University's mission by disseminating knowledge in the pursuit of
education, learning and research at the highest international levels of excellence.

www.cambridge.org

This American English edition is based on *Grandad's Magic Gadgets*,
ISBN 978-8-483-23522-5 first published by Cambridge University Press in 2009.

First published 2009
American English edition 2010

20 19 18 17 16 15 14 13 12 11 10 9 8

Printed in Malaysia by Vivar Printing

ISBN 978-0-521-14897-9 Paperback American English edition

No character in this work is based on any person living or dead.
Any resemblance to an actual person or situation is purely accidental

Illustrations by Mikela Prevost

Audio recording by hyphen

Exercises by Peter McDonnell

Contents

People in the story

Marvin: a thirteen-year-old schoolboy
Tyson: a bully at Marvin's school
Grandad: Marvin's grandpa
Mom: Marvin's mom
Principal: the man in charge of Marvin's school
Fraser: a new student at Marvin's school

BEFORE YOU READ

1 Look at the cover and the pictures in the first two chapters. Answer the questions.

1 Who are the main characters in the story?

....

2 Can you see three things that Grandad has made?

....

Chapter 1

Escape from bed

"It's happening again, Mom," Marvin shouted.

There was no reply.

Marvin was going to be late for school and it was all because of Grandad. Grandad and his crazy[1] gadgets[2].

Marvin looked up at the clock on his bedroom wall. The clock was one of Grandad's crazy gadgets. It didn't say: "A quarter after eight" which was the real time. It said "A quarter after shower time" because Marvin usually took a shower at eight o'clock. Marvin shouted again.

"Mom. Can you help me? I can't get out of bed."

Still no reply from downstairs. Marvin slowly counted to ten and then screamed as loudly as he could, "HELLO. CAN ANYBODY HEAR ME?"

Nobody could. Grandad was making too much noise in the garage. He always made a lot of noise when he was making his gadgets.

Marvin's bed was another of Grandad's crazy gadgets. Every morning at eight o'clock, the bed woke up and tidied the blankets so Marvin didn't have to. The problem was that today Marvin woke up at a quarter after eight, so the bed tried to tidy him up[3], too.

The blanket on the bed didn't want to let him go, so he couldn't move his arms and legs. He was like a banana, waiting for someone to come and eat him or like toothpaste in a tube, waiting for someone to push him out.

"Am I more like a banana or toothpaste?" he thought.

A quarter after breakfast time

Marvin could not decide which, but he knew that this was a very important question.

He closed his eyes. "Maybe I'm more like a banana in a toothpaste tube or maybe toothpaste in a banana peel. Mmm, banana toothpaste—"

"Marvin, get up. It's time for school."

Mom's loud voice ended Marvin's daydreams about fruit toothpaste. She was calling him from the kitchen.

"But Mom …" he shouted.

She didn't hear him. The clock now said "A quarter after breakfast time," and Marvin decided to try again to get out of bed.

"One, two, three, pull," said Marvin, as he tried to pull his arms out from under the blanket. But the blanket did not let him go.

"One, two, three, push," said Marvin, as he tried to push the blanket away with his feet. But the blanket still did not let him go.

He couldn't do it. The bed was stronger than he was.

"I think I'll go back to sleep," thought Marvin. "It's better than going to school."

Marvin didn't really like school these days. Tyson was at school and he was a big bully[4]. And Tyson liked to bully Marvin more than anyone else at school. Yes, it was better if he stayed in bed. He closed his eyes.

"Marvin, you're going to be late for school."

Mom's voice was loud and angry. Marvin heard her coming upstairs. Then his bedroom door opened and she was standing in front of him.

"Get up now, Marvin!"

"I can't," cried Marvin. "The bed woke up at eight o'clock

and tidied the blankets. I was still sleeping, so it tidied me, too! Now I can't get out."

"Oh, Marvin. Not again."

Mom quickly started to pull at the blankets. She could not move them.

"Let my son go!" she shouted at the blankets. "You can stay in bed all day but he can't. He has to go to school."

"Talking to them won't help, Mom," said Marvin quietly. "You have to turn them off at the wall."

Mom pushed a button next to Marvin's bed. As soon as she did this, the blankets let Marvin go.

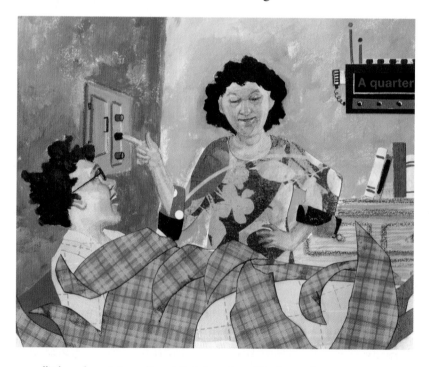

"Thanks, Mom," said Marvin. "I thought I was never going to escape."

"Why didn't you shout for help?"

"I did. Nobody heard me."

"Sorry, sweetie," said Mom. "I can't hear anything downstairs. Your grandpa is making things in the garage again and the noise is terrible."

"Since Grandad[5] moved here from England, it's always noisy," replied Marvin, just as the clock changed to "Walk to school time."

Marvin looked out of his bedroom window. He could see Grandad working in his garage. He was pulling the front off Mom's old TV! Marvin watched with his mouth open as Grandad started to hit the TV with his big hammer. Pieces of glass and old TV were flying all around the garage.

"He's trying to help us, Marvin. You know that," said Mom, as Marvin moved quickly away from the window. "It's just that ... well ... it's just that the gadgets aren't always very good, are they? Like your bed—"

"Which stops me from getting up," Marvin finished her sentence.

"Or the clock—" Mom continued.

"Which can't tell the time," Marvin said.

"Or the singing shower—"

"Which has a terrible voice."

"Or the toilet—"

"Which talks to you all the time."

Soon Marvin and his mom were laughing.

"Life is more fun now that Grandad is living here," said Marvin.

"That's true," said his mom. "Oh, and Marvin ..."

"Yes, Mom."

"Stop reading in bed. That's why you woke up late this morning."

"How did you know?" asked Marvin.

"Moms know everything," his mom replied. "And you were still wearing your glasses when you woke up." She smiled at him. "Now, get ready for school or you really will be late."

"Can I wear my new sneakers?" Marvin asked.

"If you promise[6] to keep them clean."

"Thanks, Mom," smiled Marvin, who felt that the day was better already.

But as he left his bedroom that morning, wearing his new sneakers, he didn't see that the clock was now saying "DANGER TIME!"

Chapter 2

Tyson the terrible

When Marvin arrived in the kitchen, Grandad was sitting at the table, drinking coffee and smiling a big smile. His hair was gray and his face had lots of lines on it, but he looked very young when he smiled. And he was almost always smiling.

Today he was wearing a big hat with five different pairs of glasses all around it. Grandad needed different glasses for different things. He needed them for reading, for looking at people, for using the Internet, for sitting in the sun and, of course, for making things. When he needed to change his glasses, he just turned his hat to the left or the right. So he never lost his glasses like other grandpas sometimes did.

"Good morning, Favorite Grandson!" Grandad said as Marvin quickly ate his breakfast. "You're in a hurry this morning!"

"I woke up late," said Marvin. "The bed didn't let me get up."

But Grandad didn't hear him. He was already walking to the garage and thinking about making his next crazy gadget. "Have a great day at school," he shouted as he left.

"Bye, Grandad," smiled Marvin. "Have a great day in the garage."

Marvin left home feeling happy. He was listening to his favorite music on his MP3 player and he was wearing his new sneakers.

"And I have swimming class later. I love swimming. Today is going to be a good day," he thought.

He danced along the street to the music.

"Hey, Marilyn!"

Tyson's voice cut through Marvin's happiness like a knife. Marvin knew it was Tyson because his voice was very loud and because he always called Marvin by a girl's name. Tyson thought this was funny.

"What's wrong with you, Marilyn?"

Marvin stopped his little dance and started to walk quickly toward school.

Tyson followed him.

"Hey, Marilyn. I'm talking to you," Tyson said behind him.

Tyson pushed his finger into Marvin's back. Marvin turned to look at him. Tyson was smiling but it wasn't a nice smile.

"Didn't you hear me, Marilyn?"

"I thought you were talking to somebody else. My name's *Marvin*," he replied. "And anyway, I was listening to my music."

Tyson took Marvin's MP3 player from him and listened. "What's that? Classical music?" he laughed.

Marvin looked down at his feet and tried to think of something to say. Tyson looked down at the same time.

"Ah," he said. "Were you dancing in your little new sneakers?"

Marvin found his voice. "I wasn't dancing. I was doing my fighting practice."

"Little Marilyn can fight?" Tyson laughed in Marvin's face. "Don't talk to me about fighting. See this scar?"

He showed Marvin his arm. It had a big long line on it with lots of smaller lines across it.

"Yes," said Marvin. He knew what Tyson was going to say next.

"I got this when I stopped five robbers from robbing a bank. I'm not afraid of anyone or anything."

"You said there were three robbers last time," Marvin said. He quickly took his MP3 player back from Tyson and started to run away.

But Tyson was already leaving. Some other students were coming toward them and he knew that they always watched out for Marvin.

"Be careful today, fighting boy," he shouted as he left. "I'll be right behind you."

Marvin was so angry that he got a stomachache. Tyson always made him feel bad. And every time that Tyson was bad to Marvin, Marvin's stomach hurt.

* * *

Classes in the morning were boring, but after lunch, Marvin had swimming. Marvin got ready in the locker room at school and put his bag, clothes, and new sneakers in his school locker. As he locked his locker, Tyson came in. He was right behind Marvin. Marvin quickly took his towel and ran out of the room. He didn't want anymore trouble[7] from Tyson.

Tyson looked around him. There was no one in the locker room – no one to bully. He was just leaving when he saw some keys in one of the lockers – Marvin's locker.

"Excellent," thought Tyson as he opened the door.

Inside were Marvin's bag, clothes, and … his new

sneakers! Tyson quickly took the sneakers out and closed the door again. Then he put Marvin's key in his pocket.

A few minutes later, he was standing outside the swimming pool and waving at Marvin through the window. Marvin wasn't wearing his glasses and his eyes were full of water, so he couldn't see what was in Tyson's hand at first. He climbed out of the swimming pool, dried his eyes, and put his glasses on. Then he saw everything.

"No!" shouted Marvin. "Not my nice new sneakers."

He put his towel around him and ran outside as quickly as he could. He knew he was quicker than Tyson but, of course, Tyson was wearing shoes and Marvin wasn't.

Marvin was wet and cold and his feet were hurting, but soon he could see Tyson, who was running toward the school cafeteria.

"Oh, no!" thought Marvin. "I think he's going to throw my sneakers in the trash[8]."

He was right. When he got to the cafeteria, he saw Tyson throwing his sneakers into the trash outside the school kitchen. His nice sneakers were now under vegetables, tomatoes, old pieces of meat, and fish. Marvin quickly pulled them out but they were not clean now. No. Now they had pieces of food on them and were very, very dirty.

Tyson thought this was very funny.

"Hey, Marilyn!" he shouted. "You have very dirty feet. Your sneakers were clean this morning!"

Marvin thought he was going to cry.

Tyson put his hand over his nose and came across to Marvin.

"Your feet are very smelly[9], too. Your sneakers smell like old fish!"

He ran away, still laughing.

Marvin was very angry now, so his stomach was hurting again. He wanted to run after Tyson and fight him. But he knew that was stupid. He was smaller than Tyson and he was also wet and wearing only a towel. He started to walk slowly back to the locker room in his dirty sneakers.

As he turned the corner, he saw Tyson again. The bully was standing in the playground. He wasn't moving. There was a big, angry dog outside the school gates. It was jumping up and down and making a lot of noise. Marvin could see that Tyson's face was very white. He was shaking[10] all over and holding his stomach. As Marvin got closer, Tyson's face changed from white to green and then he threw up[11] all over his shoes.

"So, Tyson is afraid of something," thought Marvin as he walked away. "And I'm not the only person who has to clean his shoes tonight."

LOOKING BACK

1 Check your answers to *Before you read* on page 4.

ACTIVITIES

2 Match the two parts of the sentences.

1 Marvin doesn't like school because ☐ *c*
2 Marvin and Mom are happier now because ☐
3 Marvin is happy today because ☐
4 Marvin's new sneakers are smelly because ☐

a Grandad is living with them.
b Tyson threw them in the trash.
c Tyson is mean to him.
d he has swimming class.

3 Complete the sentences with the names in the box.

Marvin (x4)   Tyson   Grandad (x2)   Mom

1 _Marvin_ doesn't have to make his bed.
2 .... helps Marvin escape from his bed.
3 .... has new sneakers.
4 .... makes a lot of noise in the garage.
5 .... makes crazy gadgets.
6 .... has a very loud voice.
7 .... listens to classical music on his MP3 player.
8 .... can run faster than Tyson.

4 Are the sentences true (*T*) or false (*F*)?

1 Marvin takes a shower at seven o'clock. F
2 Grandad made Marvin's bed. ☐
3 Marvin wears his new sneakers to go to school. ☐
4 Grandad doesn't need to wear glasses. ☐
5 Tyson calls Marvin "Marlon." ☐
6 Tyson takes Marvin's new hat. ☐
7 Tyson is bigger than Marvin. ☐
8 Marvin feels sick when he sees an angry dog. ☐

5 Answer the questions.

1 Why doesn't Mom hear Marvin calling her?

....

2 What does Marvin's shower do?

....

3 What does Tyson tell Marvin about his arm?

....

4 What happens to Marvin when Tyson is mean to him?

....

LOOKING FORWARD

6 Check (✓) what you think happens in the next two chapters.

1 Grandad puts a gadget on Marvin's sneakers. ☐
2 Grandad cleans Marvin's sneakers. ☐
3 Grandad buys Marvin new sneakers. ☐

Chapter 3

The sneakers talk too much

Marvin woke up at "A quarter to shower time." The bed was still asleep, so he got up quickly.

He heard his mom and his grandpa talking together, but he could hear another voice, too. Who was visiting this early in the morning?

He quickly ran into the bathroom to get ready.

"Good morning, Marvin," said the toilet. "Nice to see you again."

"Nice to see you, too," said Marvin. He always felt very stupid talking to a toilet.

"Standing or sitting, sir?"

"Standing, please," said Marvin and the toilet seat went up.

"Thank you," said Marvin when he finished. Then he turned the shower on.

"La–la–la–la–la, la–la–la–la–la." The shower started singing in a loud and very bad voice.

Marvin stood under the shower. He turned the water from "cold" to "hot."

"Oh–oh–oh–oh," sang the shower in a higher, but still very bad, voice.

Marvin put his fingers in his ears, but he could still hear the terrible noise, so he took his shower very quickly. Then he put his clothes on and hurried to see who was in the kitchen. But when he got there, he could see only Mom and Grandad. Mom was doing the dishes. Grandad was sitting at the kitchen table, drinking coffee and wearing his usual hat. Today Grandad was also wearing his "gadget jacket." It was big and red and had pockets all over it. The pockets were full of tools for making things. Marvin didn't know the names of most of them. Grandad usually wore his gadget jacket when he was making something new.

"Good morning, Favorite Grandson!" Grandad smiled his big smile.

Marvin smiled back. "Who were you talking to just now, Grandad?"

"I was talking to your new sneakers," said Grandad and he opened a box on the kitchen table.

Marvin looked into the box. They were his *old* sneakers, but they looked different. They each had a big red button on the end. Marvin took one of the sneakers from the box.

"Don't push that button!" shouted Grandad.

Too late. The sneaker shouted "Get off!" very loudly and Marvin dropped[12] it on the floor.

Grandad picked the sneaker up[13] and pushed the button again. The sneaker stopped shouting.

"Push that button when you take your sneakers off," Grandad said. "Then if someone else takes them, they will shout for help. See?"

Grandad pushed the red button on the second sneaker. It shouted "Stop! Help!"

Grandad smiled and gave the sneakers back to Marvin.

"They won't talk while I'm wearing them, will they?" Marvin asked.

"Only if you push the buttons," Grandad replied.

"These are great, Grandad. Thank you," said Marvin. He kissed his grandpa and his mom, and left for school.

Before his swimming class Marvin put the sneakers with his other clothes in the locker, but he couldn't find his locker key. "Oh well," he thought. "They'll be safe now." He pushed the red buttons, shut the locker door, and went for his swim.

A few minutes later, Tyson walked into the locker room. He still had Marvin's locker key in his pocket, but he saw that the door was already open.

"This is too easy," he smiled to himself, as he took the shoes from the locker. But he soon stopped smiling.

"Get off!" shouted one of the sneakers.

"Help!" shouted the other sneaker.

Tyson was so surprised that he dropped the sneakers. He also dropped his water bottle and water went all over the sneakers. He pushed them back into the locker and locked it with Marvin's key.

The sneakers were very wet. They stopped shouting for a few seconds. Then something went very wrong.

"It's dark in here," said one sneaker, "I'm afraid."

"Me too," said the other sneaker.

"Let me out!" shouted the first sneaker.

"Let me out, too!" shouted the other sneaker.

At that moment, the principal walked by.

"Hello!" shouted the sneakers, together this time.

"Hello," replied the principal. "Who's there?"

"We want to get out!" shouted the sneakers.

"We? We? How many of you are in there?" asked the principal as he tried to open the locker door.

"Help!" shouted the sneakers again.

Now lots of students were standing around and watching.

"Move away!" said the principal. "There are two students in the locker. I'm going to break the door and get them out!"

At that moment, Marvin came into the locker room wearing only his towel.

"What's happening?" he asked another boy.

"There are students in that locker," the boy replied.

Marvin pushed through the students. At that moment,

the principal pulled the door off the locker.

"That's *my* locker!" shouted Marvin.

"And are these your sneakers, Marvin?"

The principal had a very wet pair of sneakers in his hand. The sneakers were still talking, but much more quietly now.

"That's better," said one sneaker.

"Yes, that's much better. Thank you!" said the other sneaker.

"Yes, they're mine," Marvin said quietly. "But I don't know how they got wet."

"Your sneakers are talking," said the principal.

"Yes. Sorry."

"Sorry? Sorry? That's not good enough. I think you need to write an essay."

"An essay?" said Marvin. He knew things were bad. The principal only asked students to write an essay when they were in big trouble.

"Yes, I want you to write five hundred words about 'Why shoes are for walking, not for talking.' And I want you to put it on my desk tomorrow morning."

The other students were leaving. There was nothing more to see. Marvin pushed the red buttons on his wet sneakers, but they didn't stop talking.

"I'll have to walk home in them. I'm sure they'll stop when they are dry." Marvin thought.

But the shoes didn't stop talking. Oh, no. All the way from the school to his house, the shoes talked and talked and talked.

"Another one of Grandad's crazy gadgets," Marvin said to himself, unhappily.

Chapter 4

Marvin the rock star

When Marvin got home that night, he went to the garage. He could see Grandad through the open door. He was moving around the garage in a very strange way. Was he dancing?

"Grandad," he shouted.

Grandad waved at Marvin. "I'm sorry. I can't hear you. I'll take these glasses off."

Marvin didn't understand how taking your glasses off could help anyone hear, but Grandad wasn't just anyone.

"Now then, Favorite Grandson. What can I do for you?"

"You can stop my sneakers from talking all the time," said Marvin and he told Grandad about his day at school. "And now I have to write five hundred words about why shoes are for walking, not for talking."

"I'm sorry, Marvin," said Grandad sadly. "I was only trying to help."

"I know and I love your gadgets," Marvin said quickly. But he was just being nice. He didn't like it when Grandad was sad.

"Good!" shouted Grandad with a smile. "Because these are for you."

He gave Marvin the glasses.

"But these are just my old glasses," said Marvin. "I have new ones now."

"Yes, but I changed a few things," said Grandad excitedly. "Put them on."

Marvin thought Grandad was crazy, but he put the old glasses on.

"Now, push the button on the nose."

Marvin pushed a small button on the nose of his glasses and in a second, his head was full of music. Wonderful classical music. He soon forgot about Tyson. He forgot about the sneakers. He forgot about his essay. The music was not just inside his ears, but inside his head, his hands, and his feet. He felt wonderful.

Then Grandad took the glasses off Marvin's head and everything went back to normal again.

"You push the nose of the glasses to turn it on and off, the left side to make it go louder and the right side to change the music – from classical to rock."

"I'll never change the music," said Marvin.

"OK. But remember, 'Nose – on, nose – off, left – loud, right – rock.' Yes?"

"Nose – on, nose – off, left – loud, right – rock," Marvin repeated. "I understand. Thank you, Grandad."

Grandad smiled his big smile. "You're welcome,[14] Favorite Grandson."

*　*　*

At lunchtime the next day Marvin was sitting outside, eating his sandwiches and reading a book. His essay was on the principal's desk and he was happy with life. He pushed the nose of his glasses and beautiful music came into his ears and right through his body. He closed his eyes and his head moved slowly from side to side. He felt great. He was enjoying the music so much that he didn't see Tyson running by with a soccer ball.

BANG! – the ball hit Marvin on the left side of his head. Left was for loud, so the music got louder. Marvin jumped up and saw Tyson a few meters away. He was laughing.

"I shouted 'Catch.' Can't you hear me?" he said.

But Marvin couldn't hear him because the music was very loud now.

He wanted to throw the ball back, but his body couldn't do it. The music was loud and strong and it was inside his body. His arms and legs were moving to the music. His feet were jumping up and down and his head was moving from side to side.

"Nose – on, nose – off," thought Marvin, trying to push the button on his nose. But his hands waved around his head. "Nose – on, nose – off," Marvin tried again but his hand hit the right side of his glasses.

"Oh, no! Right is for rock music!" thought Marvin.

Two seconds later, his body was still moving to the music but much, much faster. His arms and legs danced when the guitar made a noise. His head moved when the keyboard played. His body jumped and danced and turned around to the music. He was still trying very hard to take his glasses off so he could stop dancing. But his hands were enjoying the music and they were not interested in helping him.

The other students watched him with their mouths open.

"Look at Marvin," they were saying. "He's a really good dancer. He looks like a rock star."

Then they all decided to do the same. Soon the playground was full of children jumping and waving their arms and dancing.

Then the principal arrived. Marvin's classmates stopped dancing. Marvin, of course, didn't. He couldn't.

The principal shouted at him. Marvin waved his arms.

The principal stood in front of him. Marvin jumped up and down.

The principal shook his finger at him. Marvin shook his head from side to side.

Everyone watched as Marvin shook his head. Up and down. Left and right. Marvin was shaking his head so much that … ah, at last … his glasses fell off.

No more music. No more keyboards. No more guitars. No more noise. Just the sound of the principal saying, "Marvin. I want you to write another essay. One thousand words on 'Why I am a student not a rock star.' Put it on my desk before your math test on Friday."

One thousand words! And all because of Grandad's crazy gadgets. Marvin was very angry.

He became even angrier as he sat in his bedroom later that night writing his essay. His hands were hurting and he was tired, so he was making lots of mistakes.

He looked at the clock. "Two hours after bed time," it said.

"OK. That's it. I've had enough," he said to himself.

He went downstairs to the garage and left a note[15] for Grandad. It said:

Write an essay of one thousand words on "Why I have to stop making stupid gadgets for Marvin."

Then he went to bed, still feeling very angry.

LOOKING BACK

1 Check your answer to *Looking forward* on page 21.

ACTIVITIES

2 Are the sentences true (*T*) or false (*F*)?
1 The toilet talks to Marvin. ☐T☐
2 Mom is cooking in the kitchen. ☐
3 Grandad was talking to Marvin's mom in the kitchen. ☐
4 Marvin leaves his sneakers in the classroom. ☐
5 Tyson has the key to Marvin's locker. ☐
6 The sneakers get wet. ☐
7 The principal tells Tyson to write an essay. ☐
8 Marvin's sneakers don't stop talking. ☐

3 Match the two parts of the sentences.
1 The sneakers are afraid because ☐c☐
2 The principal breaks the locker door because ☐
3 Marvin doesn't do anything wrong in the locker room, but ☐
4 Marvin puts his musical glasses on and ☐
5 The music from the glasses ☐
6 Marvin feels very angry ☐

a he has to write an essay.
b he forgets about his problems.
c it's dark in the locker.
d he thinks there are students in there.
e with his grandpa.
f makes Marvin's body move.

4 What do the underlined words refer to in these lines from the text?

1 "They'll be safe now." (page 24) _the sneakers_

2 "It's dark in here," said one sneaker. (page 25) ....

3 "And I want you to put it on my desk tomorrow morning." (page 27) ....

4 "Good!" shouted Grandad with a smile, "because these are for you." (page 28) ....

5 But Marvin couldn't hear him because the music was very loud now. (page 30) ....

6 Then he went to bed, still feeling very angry. (page 33) ....

5 Answer the questions.

1 When does Grandad wear his gadget jacket?

....

2 Who opens the locker door?

....

3 What can Marvin do with his new glasses?

....

4 What does Marvin leave for Grandad?

....

LOOKING FORWARD

6 What do you think? Answer the questions.

1 What will Grandad do when he reads Marvin's note?

....

2 Grandad invents Smelly Vision. What is it?

....

Chapter 5

What's cooking?

Marvin woke up the next morning. He was still feeling angry, but he was feeling a little bit sad, too. And he wasn't the only one. Grandad's gadgets seemed to be angry and sad, too.

Marvin looked up at his clock to see what time it was. The clock said, "Say sorry time." Marvin turned his head away. He didn't like feeling this way, but he wasn't going to say sorry because he wasn't sorry. He hated Grandad's gadgets. They got him into trouble.

Marvin's angry feet walked into the bathroom. He stood in front of the toilet. But the toilet didn't say "Sitting or standing?" this morning. It said, "Say sorry to Grandad."

"I will not say sorry to Grandad," Marvin thought. He stood under the shower and turned it on.

But the shower didn't sing loudly this morning. It sang a very slow, sad song. "S–a–y s–o–r–r–y," it sang. "S–o–r–r–y."

It seemed that all Grandad's gadgets were unhappy with Marvin – even his bed was still untidy – and deep inside Marvin knew why. He also knew that they were right. He decided he was going to say sorry to Grandad before he went to school.

He got dressed[16] and went downstairs. Mom was in the kitchen.

"Where's Grandad?" asked Marvin.

"He's in the garage. I think he's been there all night."

"Oh. Didn't he go to bed?"

"No, sweetie."

"I need to talk to him," Marvin said in a small voice.

"I think he needs to be by himself today," said Mom. "He looks very unhappy."

So Marvin walked to school with his head full of sad thoughts. His body felt heavier than usual and his legs walked more slowly.

"Hey, Marilyn!" shouted Tyson. "Not dancing today?"

Marvin didn't answer Tyson because he didn't hear him. He was thinking about Grandad.

"Hey!" shouted Tyson. He stood in front of Marvin.

Marvin looked up at the big bully and, to his surprise, he wasn't afraid of him today.

"Get out of my way, Tyson," he said.

Tyson's face changed color. For a few short seconds *he* looked afraid. Then he laughed that loud bully's laugh and said, "I'm not afraid of you, Marvin. You see this?"

He showed Marvin his arm again.

"I got this when I was fighting seven robbers, you know—"

But Marvin just walked away from Tyson. He was sick of listening to his stupid stories. Marvin sat quietly in class for the rest of the day and waited for school to finish. He just wanted to go home, say sorry to Grandad, and get the sad thoughts out of his head.

*　*　*

When Marvin got home, the garage door was still closed. So he sat in his bedroom and tried to write his essay. Because he was feeling bad about Grandad, he was making even more mistakes than usual. It was taking a long time and his hands were hurting as much as his heart.

"Marvin. Your TV show is starting," his mom shouted up the stairs.

Marvin ran into the living room. His grandpa was watching TV.

"Hello, Favorite Grandson," said Grandad.

"I'm so sorry, Grandad," Marvin replied and he put his arms around him.

Grandad smiled at Marvin and everything in life seemed OK again. Marvin's feet weren't angry, his body wasn't heavy, and his head was full of happy thoughts again.

Marvin's favorite cooking show was starting.

"Today I'm making chocolate cake," said the chef on the TV. Marvin watched carefully as the chef started to make the cake. Suddenly, Marvin thought he *could smell* chocolate. He sniffed[17] the air. Yes, he *could* smell chocolate!

He ran into the kitchen to see if his mom was making a cake, but she was reading a magazine. He ran back into the living room. The smell of chocolate was getting stronger and Grandad's smile was getting bigger.

"What's happening?" Marvin asked his grandpa.

"Welcome to Smelly Vision," said Grandad. "I finished working on it last night. Now you can watch TV and smell it at the same time."

"What!" said Marvin. "How can you smell a TV?"

Grandad smiled. "You smell what you see. There is a special button so you can make the smell stronger or weaker, just like the sound. The chef is making chocolate cake, so you can smell chocolate now, but if you watch something else, the smells change."

Grandad changed the channel on the TV. It was a show about gardens. At that moment, the room filled with the smell of grass and flowers.

"And if you don't like the smell, you can just turn it off," he said. And he pushed another button. The smell of grass slowly went away.

"This is fantastic," said Marvin. "I'm sorry I said your gadgets were stupid. I *love* them."

"Good," said Grandad, "because I have another one for you."

He gave Marvin a small white piece of plastic. "It's an eraser," he said. "You can use it when you're writing your essay. It will take the mistakes away."

"But, Grandad, I already have an eraser," Marvin said. He didn't understand.

"Ah, but you don't have an eraser like this one," said Grandad. "Watch."

He wrote some words on a piece of paper and put the eraser on the table. "Eraser," he said. The eraser started moving across the paper and taking the words away. "Stop," said Grandad and the eraser stopped moving.

"Thank you very much, Grandad. It's just what I need."

Marvin ran up to his bedroom feeling really excited. Yesterday, Grandad's gadgets brought him nothing but problems, but now he thought they were wonderful. He looked at his new eraser before he put it with the pencils in his backpack[18].

"You're going to change my life," he said.

And he was right. But not in the way he hoped.

Chapter 6

Losing words and finding friends

Marvin felt very happy when he got up. He wasn't angry with Grandad anymore. He had a wonderful TV that you could smell and see at the same time. And he finished his essay last night. It was much quicker with the new eraser.

Even thinking about the math test today didn't make him feel bad. He hated math and he hated tests. But today he wasn't going to have a problem if he made mistakes, because he could just say "Eraser" very quietly and start again. Yes, today was going to be a great day.

His clock said "lots of time to get ready" so Marvin spent a long time in the bathroom. The shower sang its usual loud and happy song in its terrible voice and the toilet was speaking to him again.

He didn't meet Tyson on the way to school, so when the math test started, Marvin was feeling really good.

Grandad's eraser worked very well. Every time that Marvin made a mistake, he said "Eraser" very quietly and the eraser moved across the page until the mistake went away. When he wanted it to stop erasing, he said "Stop" very quietly and the eraser stopped. Marvin finished the test quickly. He felt very happy with himself when the teacher told the class to stop writing and he had no more questions to answer.

Just then, the principal walked into the class. He had a small, fair-haired boy with him.

"We have a new student at the school," said the principal. "It is his first day at school today and I want you all to meet him."

Marvin liked the look of this new boy. "Who knows? Maybe we could become friends," he thought to himself.

The principal was still talking. "He is going to sit next to … Marvin."

"Yes!" thought Marvin.

"And his name is Fraser."

"Fraser" sounded like "Eraser", so the eraser started moving on Marvin's desk. But Marvin was still looking at the new boy. He didn't see the eraser as it quietly started its work.

"Maybe Fraser can come to my house for dinner and watch Smelly Vision," Marvin thought. He smiled and looked down at his test paper.

Suddenly he felt very sick. His face turned very white – almost as white as his test paper. Marvin couldn't believe it. Where were his first five test answers? He quickly shouted "Stop" at the eraser. The eraser stopped moving.

"What did you say, Marvin?" The principal looked at him.

"Umm … nothing, sir," Marvin said quietly.

The principal looked at him for a long time before he started to talk again. "As I was saying, Fraser has just moved to this town and—"

Again, the eraser heard "Eraser," not "Fraser," and started its work again.

"Stop!" shouted Marvin. The eraser stopped. The principal stopped.

"Did you shout 'Stop' at me, Marvin?" asked the principal angrily.

"No, Principal. Not at you. At my eraser."

Everyone in the class started laughing. Everyone except the principal.

"You shouted 'Stop' at your eraser? Your sneakers talk and your glasses play music. And now you tell me you shout at your eraser? Don't be stupid, boy, or I'll give you another essay to do."

"Sorry, sir," said Marvin quickly. He really didn't want another essay to write. His hands were still hurting after last night. He looked down at his test paper. Now there were only a few answers on the page.

"So, I want everyone to say a big 'Hello' to Fraser," the principal said.

Everybody in the class shouted "Hello, Fraser," and the rest of Marvin's answers went away in two seconds. Marvin put his head on his desk. He wanted to cry.

"Marvin?" The principal was looking down at him. "Move your things so that Fraser can sit next to you."

The principal picked up Marvin's test paper. He looked

at the front and then he looked at the back. There were no answers anywhere.

"You haven't answered any questions!" he shouted. "Why not?"

Marvin knew the principal wasn't going to believe him, so he said nothing.

"I don't know what's wrong with you, Marvin," said the principal. "You have changed in the past few weeks. Come and see me in my office later."

"Yes, sir," Marvin replied sadly.

Fraser smiled a friendly smile. "Too bad![19]" he said quietly.

Marvin smiled back.

"Can I have lunch with you?" asked Fraser. "I want to hear all about your talking sneakers and your musical glasses and ..." he picked up Marvin's eraser, "... why you talk to your eraser."

So Marvin and Fraser went to the school cafeteria and, at lunch, Marvin told Fraser about Grandad and his gadgets. Fraser thought they sounded great. Marvin also told him about what happened when the gadgets went wrong. Fraser thought this was very funny.

"But Smelly Vision is wonderful," said Marvin and he told Fraser all about his TV. "It's really good when you are watching cooking shows," he said.

"I love cooking," said Fraser.

Marvin couldn't believe that Fraser liked the same things that he did. Could he ask Fraser to come over to his house?

"The *Food Around the World* show is on TV tonight," he said.

"Oh. I love that," said Fraser. He looked a little shy. "Could I watch it at your house so I can smell the food while I'm watching?"

"Of course," said Marvin with a smile, and he stood up from the table and walked back to class with Fraser.

A few seconds later, Tyson moved from behind the cafeteria curtains.

"Grandad's gadgets?" Tyson said to himself. "Smelly Vision? This sounds very interesting."

LOOKING BACK

1 Check your answers to *Looking forward* on page 35.

ACTIVITIES

2 Complete the sentences with the names in the box.

> Fraser (x2)   Mom   Grandad   Marvin (x4)

1 *Marvin* is sad on his way to school.
2 .... says sorry to Grandad.
3 .... is reading a magazine.
4 .... invents a special TV.
5 .... uses a magic eraser for his test.
6 .... is a new student at school.
7 .... wants to cry.
8 .... says that he loves cooking.

3 Put the sentences in order.
1 Grandad shows Marvin Smelly Vision. ☐
2 Marvin tries to write his essay in his bedroom. ☐
3 Marvin decides to say sorry to Grandad. ☐1☐
4 The principal is angry with Marvin. ☐
5 The principal brings a new boy into the class. ☐
6 Marvin takes his math test. ☐
7 Tyson hears about Smelly Vision. ☐
8 Marvin and Fraser have lunch together. ☐

4 Underline the correct words in each sentence.

1 Grandad is in the garage because he *feels unhappy* / *is making new sneakers* / *is listening to music*.
2 Marvin goes to the living room to *do his homework* / *watch TV* / *read a book*.
3 Grandad gives *Tyson* / *Fraser* / *Marvin* an eraser.
4 Marvin has *swimming class* / *a party* / *a math test* the next day.
5 Marvin tells *Fraser* / *Tyson* / *the principal* about Grandad's gadgets.
6 Marvin and Fraser are going to *listen to music* / *play soccer* / *watch TV together*.

5 Answer the questions.

1 What does Marvin smell on the TV?

....

2 What's special about Marvin's new eraser?

....

3 Where do Marvin and Fraser go for lunch?

....

4 Where is Tyson when Marvin and Fraser are having lunch?

....

LOOKING FORWARD

6 Check (✓) what you think happens in the next two chapters.

1 Tyson breaks some of Grandad's gadgets. ☐
2 Tyson and Marvin become friends. ☐

Chapter 7

Strange sounds and smells

It was the night of the *Food Around the World* show, and everyone in Marvin's house was very excited.

Grandad was wearing both his gadget jacket and his hat tonight. The jacket pockets were full of tools. The hat was moving around more quickly than usual because he needed different glasses for all the things he was doing.

Mom was making sandwiches, drinks, and cakes in the kitchen. She was very happy that Marvin had a new friend, so she wanted to be sure that Marvin and Fraser enjoyed themselves.

Marvin and Fraser were sitting in the living room watching Grandad. Fraser thought Marvin's grandpa seemed much more fun than most grandpas he knew. When Mom walked in with the food, Grandad looked up and smiled.

"OK, boys. We're ready."

He pushed the usual button to turn the TV on and then pushed a big red button that said "Smell."

"Enjoy yourselves," he said and he left the room.

Marvin and Fraser smiled at each other. Then they both turned to look at the TV. The first chef was cooking Sunday lunch, and the smell of chicken filled the room. Marvin and Fraser sniffed the air. "Mmm, chicken," they said and they both took a sandwich.

The second chef was cooking apple pie and the smell of apples filled the room. "Mmm, apple pie," said Marvin and Fraser and they both took a cake.

The third chef was cooking pizza and they couldn't wait to see and smell that. They were very excited.

Then they heard the doorbell. Mom went to answer it. Tyson was standing there, smiling his nicest smile.

"Come in," said Mom. She thought he was another of Marvin's new friends.

When Tyson walked into the living room, Marvin couldn't believe it. He started to speak, but his mom was already talking.

"Make yourself at home, Tyson," she said. "There are sandwiches, drinks, and cake on the table."

She left, feeling happy. But Marvin and Fraser did not feel happy. Tyson put about thirty chips in his mouth.

"Move, Marilyn," he said and pushed his big body between Marvin and Fraser.

"So, this is Smelly Vision, eh?" he said as he took the remote control from Marvin's hand.

"How do you know about Smelly Vision?" asked Marvin.

"I heard you in the school cafeteria at lunchtime," replied Tyson. "When you said you had Smelly Vision, I decided to come and smell it for myself. But I don't want to watch cooking."

He pushed a button on the remote control and changed the channel.

"Ah, that's better. Soccer."

Tyson put the remote control in his pocket and started to watch the soccer game. The room became full of the smell of grass and hot dogs and hamburgers. Marvin's stomach was hurting again. He was very angry.

"Stop it, Tyson," he shouted. "You're in my house now, not at school. Give me the remote control."

"Fight me for it," smiled Tyson. "But remember how I got this …"

Tyson showed Fraser his big scar.

"I got this fighting—" he started.

"Twenty robbers. We know," finished Marvin, who decided at that moment that he was not afraid of Tyson anymore. He jumped onto Tyson and pulled the remote control away from him. Tyson couldn't believe it.

He opened his mouth to shout at Marvin but suddenly stopped. When Marvin took the remote control, he changed the channel. They weren't watching soccer anymore. They were watching a show about dogs. There were dogs all over the TV screen. Big dogs and small dogs and noisy dogs with large teeth.

Tyson was very quiet.

The room was full of the smell of dogs. The smell was in Tyson's nose and in his head. He wanted to run but he couldn't. He started to shake. His face turned white and then green. He knew that if his stomach started hurting, he was going to throw up.

Fraser didn't know what was happening, but Marvin did. He remembered the day he saw Tyson and the dog at school. Marvin was a nice boy, so he quickly changed the TV back to the food show. He thought he was helping.

But he wasn't. Now the room was full of the smell of food as well as the smell of dogs. Chicken and dog. Apples and dog. Pizza and dog. It was all too much for Tyson.

"I'm going to throw up!" he cried, as he ran from the room.

"The bathroom. Quick!" shouted Marvin.

Tyson ran to the bathroom and closed the door behind him.

"Good evening, sir," said the toilet. "Sitting or standing?"

Tyson was very surprised and he forgot to throw up. "I'm really sick," he thought to himself. "I thought the toilet talked to me." He put his hand on the wall to stop himself from falling over, and by mistake he pushed the button that turned the shower on.

"La–la–la–la," sang the shower. "Dum–di–dum–di–dum."

What was that terrible noise? Tyson put his fingers in his ears. Was the shower singing? He was feeling very scared now and he hurried out of the bathroom. He ran into Grandad.

"Are you OK?" asked Grandad. He tried to find the right glasses to see Tyson better. Tyson's eyes got bigger and bigger as Grandad's big hat turned around and around.

This was too much for Tyson.

"I don't understand what's happening!" he screamed. "I'm hearing voices and seeing things and smelling things." He ran to the front door.

"This is a crazy house!" he shouted as he ran out.

Chapter 8

Tyson tells his story

Marvin didn't sleep well that night.

Tyson wasn't nice, but Marvin felt sorry for him. Of course, he was also worried about seeing Tyson at school again.

"Oh, well," he said to himself as he got up the next morning. "It's the weekend, so I won't see him for two days."

Feeling a little better, he walked into the kitchen. But who was that at the kitchen table? No, it couldn't be. But it was. It was … Tyson!

"T–T–T–T … ?" was all Marvin could say because he was very surprised. Where were Mom and Grandad? He began to feel scared.

"He's angry about last night. He wants a fight. I have to get out," Marvin thought to himself. He started to walk back to the door.

"Morning, Marvin," said Tyson quietly.

Marvin stopped. "He called me 'Marvin,' not 'Marilyn.' What's wrong with him?" he said to himself.

Tyson was talking again, but Marvin wasn't listening. He was watching Tyson. He seemed smaller. Smaller and nicer. His body was the same. His face was the same. It was something inside that seemed different.

"I'm sorry about last night," Tyson was saying.

Marvin couldn't believe it. Tyson was being nice to him! He had to sit down.

"I'm sorry about last night and I'm sorry about being so mean to you," Tyson continued.

Marvin and Tyson sat quietly for a long time. Marvin wasn't sure if Tyson was joking. Tyson wasn't sure if Marvin believed him. They both felt very uncomfortable. At that moment, Grandad walked into the kitchen.

"Morning, Favorite Grandson," he said in a happy voice.

"Morning, Grandad," replied Marvin. He waited for Tyson to laugh at him because Grandad called him "Favorite Grandson." But Tyson just sat there.

Grandad said something quietly to Tyson and Tyson left the room.

"Where did he go?" asked Marvin.

"To the garage," said Grandad.

Marvin wanted to ask why, but first he said, "He doesn't seem like Tyson at all."

"Ah," said Grandad. "That's because he's not Tyson."

Marvin didn't understand. "What do you mean?"

"He's not Tyson. He's Lionel." Grandad said.

"Lionel?"

"Yes. His mom told me."

"When did you see his mom?"

"Last night. I was worried about Tyson because he was sick, so I followed him out of the house and walked home with him. When I met Tyson's mom, she told me everything."

"Everything?" said Marvin.

"She told me everything about Lionel."

"But who is Lionel?" asked Marvin again.

Tyson came back into the kitchen. "I'm Lionel," he said.

Tyson was now wearing a very strange blue suit. Marvin wanted to ask him about the suit, but first he wanted to hear about "Lionel."

"Lionel is my real name," said Tyson.

"But why do you call yourself Tyson?" asked Marvin.

"Because that's the name of the dog."

"The dog?"

"The dog that bit me when I was little."

Marvin looked at Grandad for help. Grandad shook his head and said, "Let Tyson tell you the story."

And Tyson did.

"When I was younger, I had a toy bear. I loved it very much." Tyson stopped talking and looked at Marvin to see if he was laughing. He wasn't.

"Well, the boy next door was a big bully. He laughed at me for having a toy bear. One day when I wasn't looking, he gave it to his dog, Tyson. I tried to get it back and the dog bit me."

"That's how you got your scar!" said Marvin.

Tyson's face became red. "Yes."

"But why do you call yourself Tyson?" asked Marvin. "That was the dog's name!"

"I decided that I wanted to be like that dog. He wasn't afraid of anything." Tyson's eyes were wet. "A bully isn't afraid of anything," he continued. "I just wanted to feel better."

"You bullied me," said Marvin quietly. "Did you feel better?"

"No," said Tyson in a small voice. "I'm sorry. I knew I was hurting you, but I couldn't stop myself."

They both felt very uncomfortable again and didn't speak for a long time.

Then suddenly Marvin said,

"So that's why you're afraid of dogs!"

"Not anymore," said Grandad, smiling his big smile. "I made him a special suit, so now dogs will be afraid of him!"

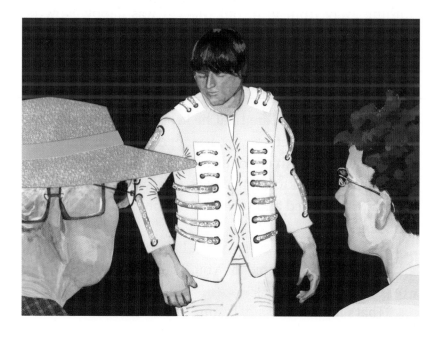

Marvin stood next to Tyson so he could see the suit better. It was very strange. It had lots of little tubes running through it with water inside. And there was a very strong smell of soap.

"What is the thing that dogs are most afraid of?" asked Grandad.

"I don't know," said Marvin.

"Baths!" shouted Grandad. "I've made Lionel a suit with bath water in it. No dog will want to come near him now."

Marvin sniffed the suit again. Yes, it really smelled of baths.

"Why don't you both walk over to Fraser's house? You can see how the suit works," said Grandad.

So Marvin and Tyson left the house. Marvin was wearing his jeans and T-shirt and Tyson was wearing his new suit.

It felt strange to be walking next to Tyson and not running away from him. But Marvin was happy. Now he had two new friends. He turned to smile at Tyson, but Tyson couldn't see him. He was looking at a big, black dog.

The dog was running toward them. It had very large teeth and it was making a loud noise. Tyson felt scared and he closed his eyes. Marvin felt scared but he kept his eyes open. When the dog was a few meters away, it stopped running and put its nose in the air. It sniffed loudly. Then it made a noise like a little baby and quickly jumped over a wall and ran away.

Marvin laughed and turned to Tyson. "It's OK," he said. "The dog's gone."

Tyson opened his eyes. "What happened?" he asked.

"The dog was scared of you," said Marvin. "The suit worked!"

"That's fantastic!" said Tyson. "I love this suit!"

He looked down at the tubes of soap and water in his jacket. "It's a little crazy," he said, "like your toilet and your shower—"

"And my sneakers and my glasses," said Marvin.

"Yes. Crazy but a little bit magic, too." Tyson said.

Marvin watched his new friend walk along in his new blue suit. Each time Tyson moved his legs, bubbles came up through the bottom of his jacket. Soon the street behind him was full of small bubbles and big dogs running away. Marvin started to laugh.

"Yes," he agreed. "A little bit crazy and a little bit magic. Just like my life since Grandad came to stay. Grandad and his magic gadgets!"

LOOKING BACK

1 Check your answer to *Looking forward* on page 49.

ACTIVITIES

2 Put the sentences in order.

1 Tyson arrives at Marvin's house. ☐
2 Marvin and Fraser watch Smelly Vision together. ☐ *1*
3 The toilet and shower talk to Tyson. ☐
4 Tyson tells Marvin why he's scared of dogs. ☐
5 Tyson changes the TV show to soccer. ☐
6 Marvin and Tyson become friends. ☐
7 Tyson says that his real name is "Lionel." ☐
8 Tyson feels sick. ☐

3 <u>Underline</u> the correct words in each sentence.

1 Fraser <u>likes</u> / *doesn't like* Marvin's grandpa.
2 *Mom* / *Grandad* invites Tyson to come in.
3 Tyson heard about Smelly Vision in the *school cafeteria* / *classroom*.
4 Tyson *feels* / *doesn't feel* afraid when the shower sings.
5 The next morning, *Tyson* / *Fraser* is at Marvin's house.
6 *Grandad* / *Marvin* talked to Tyson's mom.
7 *Marvin* / *Tyson* had a toy bear when he was younger.
8 Grandad makes a suit with *drinks* / *bath water* in it.

4 Are the sentences true (*T*) or false (*F*)?

1 Marvin and Fraser watch a food show. ⊞ T

2 Fraser takes the remote control from Marvin's hand. ☐

3 That night, Marvin doesn't sleep well. ☐

4 Mom tells Marvin that Tyson's name is "Lionel." ☐

5 "Tyson" was the dog that bit Marvin. ☐

6 Grandad says that dogs are scared of noise. ☐

7 When Tyson sees the dog coming, he closes his eyes. ☐

8 Tyson doesn't like his new suit. ☐

5 Answer the questions.

1 What show do Marvin and Fraser watch?

....

2 Where does Tyson sit?

....

3 What show does Tyson want to watch?

....

4 Why does Tyson leave Marvin's house?

....

5 How did Tyson really get his scar?

....

6 Why is Tyson's suit special?

....

Glossary

[1]**crazy** (page 5) *adjective*   stupid or not sensible

[2]**gadget** (page 5) *noun*   an object that does a particular job

[3]**tidy up** (page 5) *verb*   to put things in the right place

[4]**bully** (page 7) *noun*   a person who scares someone who is smaller or weaker

[5]**Grandad** (page 9) *noun*   British English for 'Grandpa'

[6]**promise** (page 10) *verb*   to say that you will certainly do something

[7]**trouble** (page 16) *noun*   problems

[8]**trash** (page 17) *noun*   a large container for garbage

[9]**smelly** (page 17) *adjective*   having a bad smell

[10]**shake** (page 18) *verb*   if you are shaking, your body makes quick, short movements because you are nervous or scared

[11]**throw up** (page 18) *phrasal verb*   to vomit

[12]**drop** (page 24) *verb*   to let something fall

[13]**pick up** (page 24) *verb*   to lift something by using your hands

[14]**You're welcome!** (page 30)   you say this as a polite answer when someone thanks you for doing something

[15]**note** (page 32) *noun*   a short letter

[16]**get dressed** (page 36) *verb*   to put on your clothes

[17]**sniff** (page 38) *verb*   to breathe air in through your nose in order to smell something

[18]**backpack** (page 40) *noun*   a bag that you carry on your back

[29]**Too bad!** (page 46)   you say this to someone when they are in a difficult situation

64